Bilingual Edition
Let's Get Moving™
Edición Bilingüe

The SKIPPING Book

AVANZAR A SALTITOS

Orli Zuravicky
Traducción al español:
María Cristina Brusca

The Rosen Publishing Group's
PowerStart Press™ & **Editorial Buenas Letras**™
New York

1

Published in 2004 by The Rosen Publishing Group, Inc.
29 East 21st Street, New York, NY 10010

First Edition

Book Design: Maria E. Melendez

Developmental Editor: Nancy Allison, Certified Movement Analyst, Registered Movement Educator

Photo credits: Pp. 5, 7, 18, 19, 21 by Nancy Opitz; all other photos by Maura B. McConnell.

Library of Congress Cataloging-in-Publication Data

Zuravicky, Orli.
The skipping book = Avanzar a saltitos / Orli Zuravicky ; translated by María Cristina Brusca.— 1st ed.
      p. cm. — (Let's get moving)
title: Avanzar a saltitos.
Includes index.
Summary: Pictures and brief captions describe the movements involved in skipping.
ISBN 1-4042-7515-0 (lib. bdg.)
1. Skipping—Juvenile literature. [1. Skipping. 2. Spanish language materials—Bilingual.] I.
Title: Avanzar a saltitos. II. Title. III. Series.
QP310.S45 Z87 2004b
612'.044—dc21
                                      2003009006

Manufactured in the United States of America

Due to the changing nature of Internet links, PowerKids Press has developed an online list of Web sites related to the subject of this book. This site is updated regularly. Please use this link to access the list:

http://www.buenasletraslinks.com/lgmov/avsaltitos

Contents

Contenido

I skip.

Avanzo a saltitos.

5

I skip high.

Avanzo a saltos altos.

7

I skip low.

Avanzo a saltos bajos.

9

I skip from
foot to foot.

_____

Avanzo a
saltitos
de un pie
a otro pie.

11

I skip fast.

Avanzo rápido a saltitos.

I skip in a line.

———————

Avanzo a
saltitos en
una línea.

I skip in a curve.

Avanzo a saltitos
en una curva.

I skip in a zigzag.

Avanzo a saltitos
en zigzag.

I swing my arms when I skip.

Balanceo los brazos,
cuando avanzo a saltitos.

21

I like to skip.

Me gusta avanzar
a saltitos.

23

Words to Know
Palabras que debes saber

curve
curva

fast
rápido

swing
balanceo

zigzag

Index | # Índice